Looking at All Sides

What Could Happen?

I0901367

Sonja Reyes

SOCIAL AND EMOTIONAL LEARNING FOR THE REAL WORLD™

Rosen Classroom™

How do you know what to do?

What could happen?
Look at all sides.

Think about yourself.
How would you feel?

Think about your family.
How would they feel?

Think about your friends.
How would they feel?

The best actions help everyone!

Words to Know

family

friends